CRITICAL ACCLAIM

"Iranian poet Mansour Noorbakhsh, in his defence of liberty and tolerance, in these earnest lyrics, is as unassailable as a dancing target. His verses field instigations and elegies, but always a greed for rebirth in a free space: Perhaps Canada today, but defiantly Iran tomorrow, wherever 'trees live like life itself and die like falling in love. / they don't have a tomb, their tombs are new trees.'"

— George Elliott Clarke, Parliamentary Poet Laureate of Canada (2016 & 17)

"The poems in this powerful debut collection by Mansour Noorbakhsh, enliven and redeem. His verses transport us to that magical realm of language where we can recognize each other as human and kindred. *Till You Recognize Me* is a gorgeous collection of poems brimming with fresh metaphors. We are invited to pick the forbidden fruit in an 'earthly garden planted by a storm' and to forgo the 'illusive heaven' of dogma. These verses lead us to put aside our cultural, religious, political, and philosophical dichotomies to replace them with: 'you, me and love.' The poem becomes a life-affirming, anthropomorphized entity which 'plucks' us from the tyranny of geographical and social constraints to 'replant' us in a peaceful world of belonging, understanding, and optimism."

— Josie Di Sciascio-Andrews, internationally recognized poet and host and coordinator of The Oakville Literary Cafe

"Mansour Noorbakhsh is a generational voice. At the same time intimate and expansive, his verse carries readers to places drenched in love and blood. And there, he reminds us that love is the only solvent that can wash such bloodstains from our often complicit hands. *Till You Recognize Me* belongs in the hands of readers and in libraries and classrooms across Canada and around the world."

— Darcie Friesen Hossack Commonwealth Prize-shortlisted author of Stillwater *and Managing Editor of* WordCity Literary Journal

TILL YOU RECOGNIZE ME

TILL YOU RECOGNIZE ME

Poems

Mansour Noorbakhsh

mosaic PRESS

Library and Archives Canada Cataloguing in Publication

Title: Till you recognize me poems / Mansour Noorbakhsh.

Names: Noorbakhsh, Mansour, author.

Identifiers: Canadiana (print) 20240295196
Canadiana (ebook) 20240295226

ISBN 9781771617482 (softcover) | ISBN 9781771617505 (EPUB)
ISBN 9781771617499 (PDF) | ISBN 9781771617512 (Kindle)

Subjects: LCGFT: Poetry.

Classification: LCC PS8627.O685 T55 2024
DDC C811/.6—dc23

Published by Mosaic Press, Oakville, Ontario, Canada, 2024.
MOSAIC PRESS, Publishers
www.Mosaic-Press.com

Printed and bound in Canada.

ONTARIO ARTS COUNCIL
CONSEIL DES ARTS DE L'ONTARIO
an Ontario government agency
un organisme du gouvernement de l'Ontario

Funded by the Government of Canada
Financé par le gouvernement du Canada

Canada

ONTARIO CREATES

MOSAIC PRESS
1252 Speers Road, Units 1 & 2, Oakville, Ontario, L6L 2X4 (905) 825-2130
info@mosaic-press.com • www.mosaic-press.com

CONTENTS

Dedicated to all advocates of freedom of speech

PREFACE

Sometimes a poem is like opening a door with a hard kick.

"Clumsy words" was the reaction of my dad to what I had written as a Ghazal for the first time, when I was still a student in elementary school. I just looked at him as the best reaction of a grade five student to his teacher. "Where is the soil in your poem?" he continued.

"Soil? It's a Ghazal." I replied.

"Very well, where is the water in your poem? Where are the air and the light?"

I was perplexed as he continued, "You have to work like a gardener if you want to plant a flower and it needs soil, water, air, and sunshine, right?" I had known that ancient philosophy was based on these four elements to explain nature. I had read some poems with such backgrounds and descriptions from famous poets, but it was obvious to me that such things were not considered scientific in my time.

"Soil, water, air, and fire are not substances," I said. "Substances are much more than these four things and they are quite different than these elements."

"All right, whatever substances are, we see, and we feel that any plant uses these elements to grow, thrive, and spread fragrances, so does a Ghazal." Dad said this as if he was teaching in his class for his students, then he continued, "Where is the soil of your poem coming from? Is it from a desert or from a mountain? How does water flow in it? A light rain, a flood, or a wave from a sea? What gives it light? A candle or the Sun?"

Although I did not understand what he was talking about, I could feel some taste from his words without knowing that he was trying to push me ahead like helping his child to start riding a bicycle. "Go back and first feel what you are saying and then write it down." By this sentence, he had concluded but he had known that it would take time till I really experienced love.

It is said that a book or a poem cannot stop violations in our world. But we see that love, pain, joy, and peace are similar to the wildfire that spreads from one tree to another. Therefore, this collection of poems is the result of a period of mixed affections and anxieties in the years 2020 to 2023. These poems are rooted in social events and human rights issues. They were written during the sorrowful period of the pandemic which was not an easy time for anybody. Also, in this period of time, many social issues happened in Iran, the Middle East, and other places that are reflected in these poems too. And after feeling the hard kick of human rights violations on my heart, I had no other choice but to write, till we recognize each other.

Mansour Noorbakhsh
Toronto, Canada, 2023

TILL YOU RECOGNIZE ME

Even the sky, somber or starry, needs the siren of crickets to enthrall the night. So, we may listen to it, or listen to our chanting-like paces. And still nothing can salvage a dream blown away by an irreversible sudden awakening.

Rescue a poem for me, the words of childhoods, motherhoods or loves, lost in Tehran, Baghdad or Kabul or of death in Damascus, thrown out of a hospital's window, drowned in an abandoned pool, perished in a shot down airplane or in a glorious holy jail, disappeared or abducted somewhere in the Middle East, Africa, or agitated, mortified, grieved somewhere else. And still the spell of responsibility or "justice" is a sardonic smile, the selfishness of unreal protests. Respect, regard, or sympathy in the absence of your voice is an ironic tautology. Just your subterranean words – hair-trigger landmines – threaten those who see us as staggered and silent human-like shadows. They shoot the poets. Rescue a poem and say something that keeps me dreaming of chanting-like childhood; lively, happy, and decided. Say something to rescue us from the shadow of what you see amiss and ensure we recognize each other while we are slogging along this dusty route, beside that trumpeting river, or toward that thriving meadow, as we move toward it, if we move toward it. Your silence frightens me.

JAN. 8TH

To: 167 passengers and 9 crew members perished in flight 752 Tehran on January 8th, 2020

I

At the end of loneliness
at the end of silence
at the anonymous end
of incoherence…
I haven't lived the meaning of childhood.

Spell your name
on the palm
of my hand.

As you spell it for
the blind or the deaf.

But I recognized you just
from the light you were carrying
candled in your hand in the silence.

II

How many days, weeks, and years passed
since the thunderous downing of Flight PS752, and
still cruel politicians just hiss,
in the press conferences.
But their words only
haggle away priceless lives and loves
while they bargain for
more modern weapons,
lusting for more bang
for the buck –

THE SENSE OF BEING ALIVE

The sense of being alive
is a painful need
stained with tears and blood.

The sense of being alive, is perhaps what we have called
love that invites you
to me within such lyrics.

The sense of being alive
is loneliness
the utmost loneliness
the deepest
the tenderest
that is called hope
perhaps to deceive
the inspectors and bandits.

ROCK AND ROLL OF VANISHING

Have we ever been alike?
like the bubbles
in a boat's wake

alike in swelling
alike in bursting
alike in vanishing joyfully

to mirror each other.
Without losing ourselves.

have we ever been in love
like trees?
blooming every spring
with alike blossoms,
but not ever repetitive.

trees live like life itself
and die like falling in love.

they don't have tombs;
their tombs are new trees.

DANCE LIKE FLAMES

Exhaustive as a tomb
extensive as a soul,
the lit-shallow waters
invite dolphins to lindy hop freely
like flames in a fireplace.

Dolphins tango together
enweaved as the threads of freedom moving upward
and swim back unwoven
separated in the gossamer of loneliness.

till they recircle and cuddle
again, to rise and jump
out of the water like
blazes from the ashes.

ON THE VERGE OF DOUBT

a breath of love
wafts me
from the verge of doubt.

the light you were holding
was not brighter than your eyes.

the light had always been there, anyway
what you brought to me
was how to see the light.

NATAL STREAM

before your dream
I was about to be ruined.

I'm like a tree
In the cold, I lose my leaves.

though hot summer burns
yet something runs in my deep nerves like the glow of
salmon scales in shallow water
in summer.

salmon return to
their natal stream
in autumn to spawn before dying.

within your dream
I swam toward my natal stream.

WE HAVE NOT LEFT BABYLON YET

we were told that we were ordinary and
ordinary people are good
so, we will ordinarily
will be going to heaven.

what we had
was roaring wind behind us
and destructive storms ahead
our assumptive boats
to aspired shores
cracked with the slap of
blunt wind on our faces.

yet our torn sails
could not fly us from Babylon.

we are too failed heavenly to feel alive
and too dead to fall in love,
we have become too ordinary
to merit mercy.

ORNAMENTED WITH SODA BOTTLE CAPS

your childhood was full of taste and aspiration
but you died
before experiencing lipstick.

i still remember that night
you danced away
from the eyes of others
in a special dress sewn by yourself
ornamented with soda bottle caps
an embroidered fringe
like a bridal lace dress
jingling with each sway.

you played the music of your girlhood
away from any ear
and in darkness.

THE BARE SHOULDER OF NIGHT

drunken
you look more beautiful
and recite poems more beautifully soft and lively
like rising sunshine
lighting the bare shoulder of night.

night disappears in your reciting
covers the window entirely
and your benevolence
radiates toward the horizon.

i want to drop
gently like drizzles, like dew,
on the bare shoulder of night
to become drunken.
like perfume
on a waltzing bride.

A CUP OF KISSES

A cup of kisses.
A pavilion of solitude.
I start loving myself,
When your dream survives
this loneliness of the everyday crowd.

Amidst this alienating bustle
I buy a ticket to departure
toward a poem.
A seat of cuddles.

Tell the clock to repeat your name
when it chimes for annunciation.
That's the only time the commotion fades.

Even the trace of your gaze
marking the edge of my cup
suffices for me to leave this
anxious station,
and park – to drink – at your mouth.

FORBIDDEN FRUIT

a response to the terrorist attack against Salman Rushdie

you know a barbed wire
only grows nothingness
and only protects hunger and fear.

we all were from the mass graves.
though our graves have been separated
by barbed wires,
each mass grave on one side of that,

but still, we can sing,
barbed wires never separate the songs.

ALONG THE GLASS DOOR

this poem is supposed to talk
about your character,
but i don't know you much.

it's not true too, if i say
i don't know you, since
i know how much you have changed me.

if it talks about changes you made in me,
thus it speaks about you.

let it word my grief of not knowing
how you have changed along with me.
the changes it talks about
do not affect a statue.

passing along the glass door,
like me,
you were sinking slowly, slowly
you were smoldering to ashes bit by bit.

perhaps feeling thrives like pollination
that exchanges life within living plants.

perhaps apathy is a fire that expands
from one plant to another,
whether alive or dead.

SURVIVAL

narcissus flowers
were breathing
in the warm living room
although the snow outside
was killing their roots.

someone rescued them
put the picked ones'
in a jar.

they lived a little longer
tried to pollinate normally
in each breath
though it bore no new blossom.

depicted beauty ruins survival.

BREAD AND SHAME

I open my eyes but
I do not see the world.

I see a child
dreaming of rain
in a thirsty dusty desert.

A child that has never tasted
love but shame,
impregnated with
the smell of bread.

I open my eyes and
I do not see myself.

MINE, OURS

The ignored 'me'
Dribbles out as a poem
from a melting iceberg.

Let me feel slaked
after feeling my thirst.
And touch the clouds
with my full passions.

Let me feel my earthy veins.

Eloped and unconscious
like the flakes of a blizzard
after a repetitive battle
moved to ebbs of rain.
I feel the earth, the growing
plants, drizzles, and sunshine.

The poem plucks
and replants me
somewhere that I feel
is mine, ours.

REALITY AND JUSTICE

To: 215 children found buried on the site of what was Canada's largest Indigenous Residential School.

We have been playing in darkness
with covered eyes,
since we were children,
then I wanted to find you
for I needed to win.

Children were told
darkness is reality
and for the middle-aged
covering our eyes with a dirty
handkerchief called justice.

The Morse code of victory?
Pacing in darkness with covered eyes,
touching feely with walls
then freefalling into graves.

DIGNITY

"To: Joyce Echaquan, the Indigenous woman who recorded slurs by hospital staff before her death."

A flat tire stopped us
In the middle of a vast desert
which lies between two oceans.
Sands can move through borders
freely with the wind,
as waves can move
through borders in the ocean.
No border exists for sand and waves.

Sands are equal, waves too.
We are stopped in the middle of a desert
a few kilometers away from the border,
with the dream of freedom.
Sweating and burning under
the intense sun. Dying. Thirsty.
And I think of those who drowned
in the ocean waves, a few kilometers away from a border
attempting to save their freedom,
their dignity.

Sands are equal, waves too.
But still human beings are only equal
in dying.

I WANT TO SING THE BITTEREST ROMANCES

A prayer for Afghans after brutal Taliban advance in August 2021.

The sunshine was nothing
more than a dream
in the commotion of an evening.
Call the rain which doesn't decline hopes.

I want to sing the bitterest romances
to have no one crediting any smile
and to have no one despairing for a glance.
Thus, death never expects any resurrection
and soil never promises the sprouting of
any grape vine to make us drunken.

I want to sing the bitterest romances
so that every heart embraces sin
despite a certainty that casts a shadow
Over the peace of demon glorifiers
those buyers of lies and sellers of death.

Those who see purity only
in the captivity of virgin girls
and seek faith only
in the slavery of men in love.
Those who believe selling opium
to buy weapons is permissible.
Death-Believers who
don't trust the meaning of life.

I want to sing the bitterest mourning-song,
as if infidels had not fought
but only against their own silence.

TOAST FOR BREAKFAST

This morning, a hungry I
appeared in the sleek oval surface of my toaster
deformed and staring
at the row of marching slices of bread,
uniformed in a plastic bag.

The scorched bread spread
the fragrance of sourdough
the smell of childhood.
Hungry I leaned over to smell
its identity scrambled like
a dribbling liquid on the toaster's surface,
my eyes merged
like an empty bowl.
My face turned like the globe's circle
in the breaking news.

The bread colored, blushed
warm and attractive,
with the fancy of a joyful crunch.
Closer, my lips and teeth disfigured it to a continent,
a restless city,
and then to a row of people staring at me.

The toaster screamed and the toast ejected.

MIDDLE EAST

Many years ago, a man who was selling cactus fruits
on his handcart,
red and sweet,
was peeling the fruits for his customers.

His hands were rough like cactus leaves,
He told us, "*if I don't peel the fruit,*
the thorns will hurt your hands and mouth."

There I have seen cactus and orange plants growing
side by side,
while women and children were working together.
In a hungry and thirsty land surrounded by
mountains, rivers, and seas.
Where the cradle of civilization is buried.

Now, it's said that bullets are planted there,
and bombs are the bloom.

And people have abandoned planting
the drought-resilient fruits,
and the cradle of civilization near the oil wells,
is beyond drought.

A poet imagines how the land continues growing
sweet fruit, resilient to the drought,
but I don't know whose hands will remove the thorns.

SNOWMAN

Snowman came late last night.
Slowly, slowly.
Bit by bit.
Soundlessly.
Distributed everywhere.
Belonging to all.
Not as a man or a woman.

Then he stood up,
without stealing anything.
Just wore what was left.
Happily.
And didn't call all other snowmen
together.

Later with the sunrays, snowman left us.
Again slowly, slowly.
Again soundlessly.
Returned to everywhere, like sunrays, with sunrays.

Kept his smile on his face,
until the last moment
And left all that once belonged to human beings,
like that old scarf, on the ground.

SNEAKY BUD

To all martyrs of "Women, Life, Freedom"

You were born as the children of soil,
with an unbelievable similarity to the wishes of the sun.

They turned you into dust
to leave you in the hands of wind.

Everything in their universe
should be raised under what they have dictated to God.
They have no interpretation of soil, rain, and sun.

Your only sin was a sneaky look at God's bedroom.

WHO AM I?

Heavy rain brings me to the earth.
Even the sky above me
can only be seen
when I am on the earth and I have bent my neck back.

Dry fruits are sweeter and long-lasting,
if born from heavy rains
and raised by hot sun rays.

Heavy rain washes me to the soil,
from the sky that can be seen only from the earth
while my feet have rooted in it
and my neck is bent toward the sky.

NOWRUZ 2023

For "Women, Life, Freedom"

Hyacinths need the full sun
that comes in late winter
or early spring.

What flowers will make
this year attractive to Nowruz?
Enshroud with tattered leaves,
clusters of fragrant,
schooner stiff, upright stalks,
as the growth of your hands.

Your hands will bring Nowruz this year.
You, who went to the street to bring the full sun
in a night that still wanders between
its scarlet sky of sunset and dawn.

The night that your blood uncovered.

I wait for a Nowruz that rises from your collar,
that beats with your red blood.
Hyacinths will feel the full sun then.

DROPPING SLOW

After: And I shall have some peace there, for peace comes dropping slow,
Dropping from the veils of the morning to where the cricket sings; (W.B. Yeats)

I close my eyes,
but I still can hear, unintentionally.
Like hearing the news
when you drive on a dark road.

Tired of a long run,
burdened, behind my closed eyes, I hear,
perhaps a clamorous flea market.
Your voice's visuals, not what I need.

Behind my closed eyes,
the mother turtle leaves
the shore and her buried eggs.
With tears in her eyes.

Something rustles afar.
As if baby turtles leaving the shore,
and their hatched eggshells,
in the opposite way of their mother.

FICTIONAL LIFE

no memoir is free of fiction pieces
that makes foods delicious
and warms kisses,
within thousands of photos
buried under millions of others
autographed by emojis.

today i tried to call an old friend in Iran
the voice was indistinct
i just heard, "*internet access is very poor*
we cannot even load a photo
they've turned it off
to smother us."

i load a photo, and stray around messages
again and again, in a free country
to feel fictionally alive.

then, my life turns to a question,
nonfictional.

RESKINNED MOLOCH

To: Ukrainian children after the Russian invasion

has raised again his shadow
with open arms
to burn the children,
though he has changed, reskinned,
this time.

his arms are open
to embrace the world,
Ukraine, Europe ...
what else would be the next?

perhaps i am still an immature child
who dreams of maturity in lovely world.
in every poem
innocent
unaware of the
plentiful pollen of immature cruelty
growing under the skin of
this mushroom-shaped cloud.

perhaps i am a child who
has learned and believed
Moloch is untrue
but had not known that
it can be emulated, reskinned.
or it's nothing but a skin

THE TORCH THAT WE NEVER SAW

A prayer for Afghans and Afghanistan after a brutal Taliban advance while American soldiers and diplomats are leaving Afghanistan.

The water hit us like hard rocks. The darkness swallowed us with violent waves when we heard the boat breaking and we saw the light of bullets towards our boat. The waves that we had never seen before and had not known how powerful they were to smash our weak bodies and the boards of our boat, had hit us. We had been taught that water is for liveliness. We were not familiar with the deadly waves, nor with dying in the wandering waters. With the first whistle of a bullet and with the first shake of the boat that broke, we spilled into the stormy waves. As we had been told. We had nowhere to go into, but the embrace of deadly waves. And we had learned nothing but that. And only then did we realize that what they had taught us was to die and die only. Not how to survive. On the beach, no hand was shaking any torch for us. Because no one, neither expected nor believed that we could reach the shore from such violent waves.

A CAREFREE POEM

After: "The Scream" a painting by Edvard Munch

Any scream is a loneliness
echoed in an afternoon coffee
on the patio of a survivors' café.
Waving in your eyes
looking at the shining waves
of the coffee that are
moving warm and exulted / exulting
toward the strong wall of cup
and turn back and start again
want something to happen
as you slowly turn the cup in your hand
and move your eyes around
the silent people who buy a coffee too
and take a seat apart from each other too,
looking, hoping for exulted /exulting, shining waves.

You chose metaphors
as a shelter, a parapet,
you knew how lies and daggers
are cruel together
and so, fearless lies
and unthoughtful stabs.

You invented the poem, then
as a shelter for your heart
in the days of roving loves
and you chose metaphors
spiting the famine of thoughts.
But I need to inhale a carefree poem.

AROUND THE WORLD

I

Commotion is a shattered silence__
still silent, but comprehensible.

Are all silences,
let's say shattered silences
or commotions alike?
like a puzzle with infinite parts
but all similar in shape?

Like the puzzle of city windows in the background of
the breaking news
infinite flickering spots
fill the world with similar pieces,
replicating and perplexing
piece with peace.

II

Your poem protects our differences
while the idealists' prayers sink into
the global warming of the stock market.

Come, you will find me
from a burning dance
hung up on a window
resembling your poem.

I will be waiting for you
while you are ascending
word by word.

MEET

After: "Requiem" by Anna Akhmatova
To: all martyrs of human rights.

I will never forget you
I cannot
although I know you will
not come back,
and I will
not see you again.

Where did you die?
I don't know.
Hanged in a prison
or killed in a war?

I never believed the news
that said you had committed
suicide, in a prison,
or were killed in a clash
in a street.

But I know,
I knew that from the beginning,
nothing is more bloodthirsty
than love.

PANDEMIC VS UTOPIA

The cracked eggshell of
your certainty spills viruses,
excuse me Plato
we need social distancing and
disinfecting the Forms and Ideas to pass the faith over.

The destiny of humankind, now, puzzled, loses the
intensity of an entire summer
while people must keep their distances__
but flowers are blooming
and fruits are ripening.

Let's leave Utopia to animals
and take refuge in our loneliness,
groping blindly,
by feeling the limbs of
dissected mirages,
the inexorable laws.

Still what if coincidentally
we touch the palm of a
dissected-admirable-intuition,
and an unfocused grief appears
among the feverish questions?
perhaps about our common weal.

AMEN

I need someone to dream for me
If it's impossible to dream of heaven
let it be in its very primitive shape.
With rough eyes fiercely look,
At the sweat of wine and liquor
that can be smelled from armpits.
Like the freshness of grape vines in a misty garden,
as if some galloping horses had left there:
dust, sweat and manure.

Have you ever seen yourself
as I see you? I know human beings are eager to be alive
even in slavery, in prison or other humiliations,
"I want to know if you can be alone with yourself" *

Choose either absurdity or pain.
Live without any pretext
in this giant circus.

Here I stay in the abyss of Hell
content with a drop of wine.
I can't live without failure*.
You, cleric, go and find your supposed heaven,
if it's still not ruined by love.

---

* *The Invitation by Oriah Mountain Dreamer*

THE MEANING OF JOINTS

The night,
grapples with the buttons of my garment
in the repetition of a battle between the meaning of my
fingers and the numbness of the cold.

I am not afraid of death
My fear is the repetition of death and its multiplication.
I have died many times before
in the teeth stained with blood and pain that have
repeated a single word.
Like farewell kisses.

Like chewing the cold
and the tremble of
numb fingers.
That prevents distinguishing
the buttons from the night.

FOR MAHSA AMINI

Mahsa Amini died on 16 Sep. 2022 when she was arrested by Morality Police of Iran's Government. Her death was the beginning of the "Women, Life, Freedom" movement in Iran.

There is a sign for life
and for death too.

Amid the chaos of death preachers
and the silence of us,
the victims of preaching.

The bruise of your eye is a sign that
you had known life.

You crossed the fearful border of silence
to leave the chaos of death.

And your bruise is a sign
for me this time and every time
to look deeply for the sign of life in myself.

There is a sign for death
as for life too.

Leave your hair to the wind.

IRANIAN YOUTH

For Mahsa Amini, and all martyrs of freedom

I am a generation that my days
have never tolerated in me.
I see you kill
but verbalize the justice.
I see you steal
but lament because of oppression.
I see it's foul only
what you do in the name of morality.
I find no name for you
except bandits
except tyrants.

Which crypt have you come from
that has no tolerance for sunshine?

I am a generation that
cannot tolerate the intolerance
though I have nothing but my burning heart
that rises with anger and pain
against the hypocrisy that loots
our moments.

OUR OWN DAMN STORY

We didn't start our journey together.
Our roads had never crossed
except in the missionary ships.

My father was an unknown who had become Muslim
travelled with a ship of Christian Missionaries.
Who was my mother?

Al Capone and Citizen Kane arrived together.

We arrived later.
My mother died when I was born.

My brother got a job backstage at
Citizen Kane.
And my sister in one of the laundry shops of
Al Capone.

I love to stroll with you
at dusk for window-shopping downtown
to read the cover pages of poetry books
behind the vitrines of book shops.

And posing like a poster of advertising models.

TRAPPED OR GLOWING

Like Navid Afkari who was executed on 12 Sep. 2020
for participating in protests in Iran.
To all human rights activists in Iran.

I saw dew drops on a spiderweb
glowing, in this beautiful morning.
Are they trapped,
or placed here to glow?

First thing what woke you up
in the spiderweb of social media,
was that another brave young man
is executed, is killed
because of raising his voice.

He did nothing but cry out
our rights, human rights.
Now, he is killed in favor of
real criminals, who kill and laugh,
while we were silent, asleep.

They plan executions before sunrise.

I'm beholding trapped dew drops
which will never last in the spiderweb
after the sun comes up,
but are telling me aloud,
glow as yourself,
even in your last moment.

BREWING COFFEE-POEM

My profile pictures
smile continuously
inviting you for another
click.

My phone beats as my heart
my email rings like a doorbell
for another invitation to another Zoom.

We must option
social distancing
but longing continues,
boiling a poem
while brewing a coffee
for a little rest and
a deep breath.

You taste this coffee-poem
in an electronic device
and I feel your eyes
shining
behind the screen.

RECURRING LIKE LIGHTNING

hearts hibernate in dreams
fed by roots of
desire and esteem
stay dormant till
returning like lightning

bodies get old,
fire of time ashes them,
but hearts melting
like crystals
in the crystal workshop
burning as a molten fire
twisting in a burning dance
shining, stunning thus
cools to resemble
rebellious flames
standing rogue but fragile

my heart recurs
in your fragile dream

MUSTANGS

Your dream recollects us alive.
The song of wilderness.
The run of passing time.

How have you become tamed
to resemble civility?

How have you forgotten your trotting,
and the arisen dust after galloping?

How have you ended the night
without an eager neigh
to call a mating dawn?

Where did you lose your flock?

I hope the springs you drank from still flow,
Perhaps the sprouts your colt grazed, still grow.
If your manure finds the lovely
bed of land widespread.

Your dreams embody freedom and fertility.

IF I WERE YOU

If I were a tree
you might be coming
every spring
to make a nest
out of my branches
although for
one spring and
one summer, only.

And I would come
to watch your
sprouts that hymn to
life on your stems
if you were a tree.

GRAPE HARVEST

No. Wine invaded neither
my heart
nor my eyes.

It was the realm of wine
invaded
by your smiles.

Raindrops glistened on
the grapes and
wind grappled with the grapevine.

Red, purple and green
grapes
smiled, ripening in sunshine.

My heart sweetens
in sunshine
and thrives in rain like rainbows.

Wind grapples with your hair
as if I'm running
wherever it goes.

How could drunkenness
trick me
into forgetting you, ever?

What I could only see
is your smile,
drunken and sweeter.

NOT YET FLAWED

I carry a mirror everywhere,
clean and clear, like the full Moon.
Taller and wider than myself.

Carrying it is not an easy thing,
like your love.
Even traumatic. But,
it can't be fooled
anywhere and by anyone.
It doesn't hide anything,
like your heart.

So, what do you think?
How many people can tolerate it?
How many doors may welcome it?
But I am not afraid, like your eyes.
If they spit at it
it helps me to clean it better, and more often.
And if they throw rubble at it,
demolition debris, although painful,
I'll be happy, like your smile.
I'm sure a shattered mirror
"Not yet flawed, it drifts. Pine and cinnamon
Spreading in my old garden . . . All light," *
reflects greater, even unlimited light.
And no doubt, there are many other people
ready to carry each piece of it
taller and wider than before.

---

* *Full Moon by Du Fu*

THE POET

To Allan Briesmaster

No copy resembles perfection
but more corruptive,
realism is still far from maturity,
our world still flows in our words.

The poet generously deconstructs
the world of words
to bravely breed a poem
not belonging to a specific region
or even to a specific language
but the whisper of people
among their intuitions,

the flux of reality to the dreams,
a perpetual unstoppable
destroying and rebuilding
of our childish realism.

CRACKED POMEGRANATES

I've been silent for a long time
Like that pomegranate tree
in our house
when I was a child.
A tree that never had enough water to its roots
but every spring was filled with blossoms,
and its branches full of pomegranates
every summer,
though most of them had cracked skin.

My mother said smiling,
"These are smiley pomegranates."
She was keeping some of them
for cold long winter nights
I've been silent for a long time
like my mother, my father, my siblings,
and my classmates.
Like our pomegranate tree
and other trees in our neighborhood,
which have never spoken

Share your drunken moments with me
until I drop the last drop of my life
into your glass.
Like a cracked skin pomegranate.
Sadness is nothing but a heart,
empty of a bright imagination.

Share your drunkenness with me
abandoned but enriched with
the music of the joyful tumult of
rivers, mountains, and seas
which have freely spoken
in all cold long winter nights.

THE EIGHTH DAY OF THE POET

Poem is the other name of silence
as waves of grief
and storms of desire
rise to the rocks of words
searching for the culmination of a
mesmerizing tranquility.

While the poet is ejected
from the lake of fire
to the painful and chaotic world
afraid of slaying love
by repose and silence.

ACKNOWLEDGMENTS

I hereby express my gratitude to Dr. George Elliott Clarke for reading my poems and providing his remarkable comments and edits.

Also, I owe the publication of this collection of poems to the encouragement of Josie Di Sciascio-Andrews, to whom I am very thankful for her editing as well.

PREVIOUSLY PUBLISHED WORKS AND AWARDS

Books

In Search of Shared Wishes, 2017, Canada

Mansour Noorbakhsh has also published the following two books, and several articles and poems in Persian language (Farsi).

به سراغ من اگر می آیید / زندگی وشعر سهراب سپهری

Life and Poetry of Sohrab Sepehri, Morvarid Publication, Iran

دیدار با فلق / زندگی و شعر منوچهر آتشی

Life and Poetry of Manuchehr Atashi, Jameshenasan, Iran

Poetry

- Three poems published *WordCity Lit*, October 2020, Canada
- One poem published in each issue of *Verse Afire,* the bi-annual publication of The Ontario Poetry Society, compiled and edited by I. B. Iskov, 2020, Canada
- Three poems published in *Infinite Passages*, an anthology, pp 94, 153, 155, illustrated and compiled by Katerina Vaughan Fretwell, published by The Ontario Poetry Society, 2020, Canada
- "The Poet" published in *The Celebration of Poetry*, 20th anniversary, p 60, compiled, and edited by I. B Iskov, published by The Ontario Poetry Society, 2020, Canada

- Eight poems published in *Rendezvous*, an anthology, pp 34-42, compiled by Elizabeth Barnes, published by IOWI, 2021, Canada
- Five poems published in *Consonant Lights*, an anthology, pp 25-29, compiled and edited by Josie Di Sciascio-Andrews, published by IOWI, 2022, Canada
- "Reskinned Moloch" published in *Poets for Ukraine*, Vol 2, p 15, compiled by David C. Brydges, published by Brydges Builder Press, 2022, Canada
- "If I were you" published in *Poem in Your Pocket* by Parkland Poets' Society, 2021, Canada
- "River's Reverie" published in *Outlying Voices Vol 4*, p 39, published by Parkland Poets' Society, 2022, Canada
- "untouchable invisible paths" published in *Outlying Voices Vol 5*, p 37, published by Parkland Poets' Society, Canada, 2023.
- "on the verge of doubt" translated into Macedonian and published in ЗБОРНИК НА КАРАМАНОВИ СРЕДБИ 2021 by International Karamanov Poetry Festival, compiled by Daniela Andonovska-Trajkovska, 2021, North Macedonia
- "Survival" translated into Macedonian published by *Karamanov Poetry Meetings Anthology,* compiled by Borche Panov, 2022, North Macedonia
- Five poems, an interview, and an essay translated into Slovenian, published in *Poiesis*, edited by Peter Semolic, 2022, 2023, Slovenia
- Five pieces of "In Search of Shared Wishes" translated into Italian by Claudia Piccinno, published in *Menabo*, 2022, Italy
- A poem entitled "Fellow Traveler" presented in *Rucksack* a Global Poetry Patchwork, compiled by Antje Stehn, 2021, Italy
- A poem entitled "For Mahsa Amini" published in *Cervine Barva Press channel (Hair In The Wind)*, compiled by Antje Stehn, 2023, Italy

- Three poems published in *HAPPENING Multicultural Festival,* compiled by Banoo Zan, 2023, Canada
- Several love poems translated into Spanish and aired in *UMRO*-Spanish Radio, 2021, 2022, 2023, Mexico

Awards

- "Till You Recognize Me" (poem), honourable mention in Brooklin Poetry Society's Annual Poetry Contest, 2020
- "Not Left Babylon Yet" (poem), third place in the Poems in English Language category in *PREMIO INTERNAZIONALE D'ECCELLENZA "CITTA DEL GALATEO – ANTONIO DE FERRARIS" IX Edizione – ROMA*, 2022, Italy
- Poet-in-Residence, *WordCity Lit*, 2022, Canada

BIOGRAPHY

Mansour Noorbakhsh writes poems and stories in both English and Farsi, his first language, and has published books, poems, and articles in both languages. His book-length poem *In Search of Shared Wishes* was published in 2017. He strives to be a voice for freedom, human rights, and the environment in his writing. He presents The Contemporary Canadian Poets in a weekly Ottawa Persian radio program.

Mansour's poems have been widely published in *WordCity Lit, Verse Afire, Parkland Poets*, and several anthologies. His poems have been translated into Greek, Italian, Portuguese, Spanish, Slovenian, Serbian, Macedonian, and Chinese. Mansour Noorbakhsh is an Electrical Engineer and lives with his wife, his daughter, and his son in Toronto, Canada.